This collection is dedicated to Mr. William Witkowsky, my junior high school art teacher. It was my great fortune to be his student.

NIGHT LIGHTS & PILLOW FIGHTS

A TRIP TO STORYLAND

WORDS AND PICTURES BY

Guy Gilchrist

WARNER
JUVENILE
BOOKS

A Warner Communications Company

New York

A C K N O W L E D G M E N T S

First off, I thank my good friend Tom Brenner and my wife, Mary, for their extraordinary dedication and assistance with the coloring of the pictures drawn for this collection.

Robin Corey, who helped me sift through scribbled-in composition books and choose the rhymes.

Bonnie Lang, who was a great help with the title designs and lettering.

Harry Nolan, designer, and Linda Palladino, who has an eagle eye for color proofs and makes it all happen on the printing press.

And finally, I am grateful to my daughter and son, and the children it's been my good fortune to meet all across the country this past year. Thank you for spending pieces of your childhood days humoring me and letting me tell you some silly stories.

Warner Juvenile Books Edition
Copyright © 1989 by Guy Gilchrist Productions, Inc.
All rights reserved.
Warner Books, Inc., 666 Fifth Avenue, New York, NY 10103

(W) A Warner Communications Company

Printed in the United States of America
First Warner Juvenile Books Printing: November 1989
10 9 8 7 6 5 4 3 2 1

Library of Congress Cataloging-in-Publication Data

Gilchrist, Guy.
  [Night lights and pillow fights]
  Guy Gilchrist's night lights and pillow fights : a trip to
storyland.—Warner Juvenile Books ed.
      p.   cm.
  Summary: An illustrated collection of humorous poems about
kangaroos, goblins, pogo sticks, princesses, and franks and beans.
  ISBN 1-55782-084-8
  1. Children's poetry, American.   [1. Humorous poetry.
2. American poetry.]   I. Title.   II. Title: Night lights and pillow fights.
PS3557.I34259N54   1989
811'.54—dc20
                                                88-40622
                                                   CIP
                                                    AC

TABLE · OF · CONTENTS

A RHINOCEROS ON MY HEAD

Every day I wear a rhinoceros, right on the top of my head.

And every night I take him off before I climb in bed.

I hang up my rhinoceros on the bedpost by his horn.

Then I put my rhinoceros back on my head the first thing the next morn.

OLD MR. CRADDICK

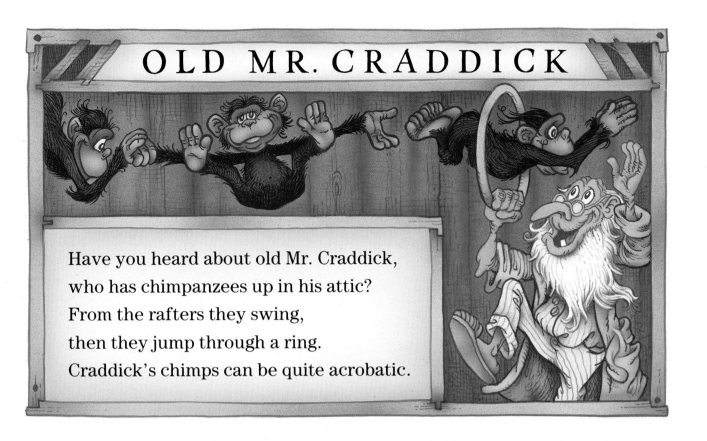

Have you heard about old Mr. Craddick,
who has chimpanzees up in his attic?
From the rafters they swing,
then they jump through a ring.
Craddick's chimps can be quite acrobatic.

A MONSTER NAMED CLARK

There once was a monster named Clark,
who scared me each day at the park.
But the park was all right;
I could play there at night.
'Cause Clark was afraid of the dark!

FRANKS · AND · BEANS

Franks and beans! Franks and beans!
Dinner of kings! Dinner of queens!
They don't like quiche or caviar,
or lobster bisque or steak tartare.
No, the only food for the royal clan
is franks and beans, right from the can!

HICKORY · DICKERY · DOCKERY

Hickory, dickery, dockery,
the mouse broke Thelma's crockery.
He broke her pans! He broke her pot!
He broke her bowls! He broke a lot!
He bent her forks! He bent her spoons!
Then he sat on her pillow
and watched some cartoons.

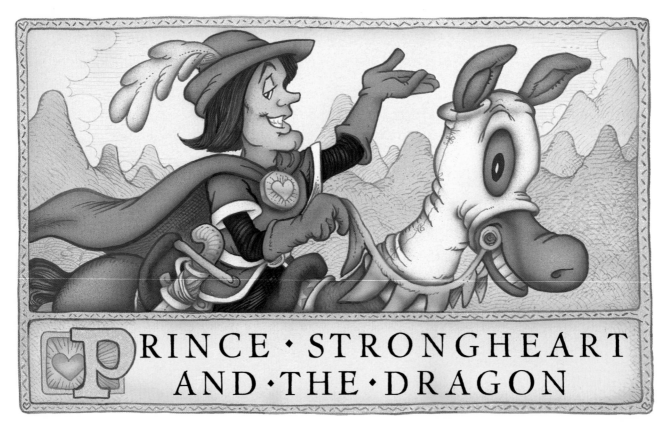

PRINCE · STRONGHEART AND · THE · DRAGON

Prince Strongheart rode on his trusty steed
in search of a place where he could do a brave deed.
He said, ''There must be a village that's in danger enough
that they'd welcome me there to save damsels and stuff.
And fight off their giants—with one head or two.
Or monsters! Or dragons! Any creature will do!
For if the village has monsters or dragons to kill,
the whole village will cheer me. I know that they will!
Their grateful king will give me his daughter so fair
and we'll live happily ever after in a kingdom somewhere.
Because,'' thought the Prince, ''that's how fairy tales go.''
So, he rode to a cliff with a village below.

Then the Prince said, "On, Steed!" and he rode into town,
shouting, "I'm a brave prince! Come and gather around!"
So the villagers gathered around this bold stranger,
and the Prince said, "I'm here to save people from danger.
Do you have any dragons you want me to smite?
Do you have any two-headed giants to fight?
If you do, I will fight them! I'm Prince Strongheart, you know!
Do you have any?" asked the Prince. All the townsfolke said, "No."
"We used to have a dragon," said a little old man,
"who'd show up breathing fire and burn up our land.
He'd spit fire from his mouth and blow smoke from his ears.
But, sorry," said the man, "we haven't seen him in years."

"Well," said Prince Strongheart, "then it's plain to see,
I'll do my deeds somewhere else. You have no need for me."
Then he mounted his steed and was waving good-bye
when the Princess, so lovely and fair, caught his eye.

 For the Prince, when he saw her, it was love at first sight.

But for *her* to love *him*, he needed something to fight.

 Then the Prince remembered the dragon the old man had spoke of.

If he could slay the dragon he could win the maiden's love.

 So he thought up a fib to announce to the crowd:

"I hear your dragon's coming back!" said the Prince, good and loud.

 "So I'm off to find this monster before he comes back!

Before he burns down your village in a dragon attack."

 To the Princess he cherished he waved his bravest wave.

Then he left on his horse for the dragon's dark cave.

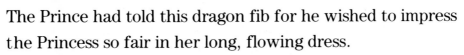

The Prince had told this dragon fib for he wished to impress
the Princess so fair in her long, flowing dress.
So now he had to find this beast, so all day long he rode
until he reached the highest peak and the dragon's dark abode.
Prince Strongheart pulled his sword out, then he crept into the lair
and there he found an old dragon, half-asleep in a rocking chair.
The old dragon looked wrinkled and tired and bored.
But his eyes opened wide when he saw Strongheart's sword!
The dragon looked at the Prince and the Prince looked at the dragon.
"Good evening!" said the dragon, his pointed tail waggin'.
"Good evening, Mr. Dragon," said the Prince to the beast.
"I've come here to slay you, or try at the least!"
"Slay me?!" said the dragon. "Why, Prince, I'm too old!
My breath once was hot; now it's quite sadly cold.
I can't blow smoke from my ears now, much less breathe some fire!
I can't fight anymore so I had to retire."

"Oh, no!" said Prince Strongheart as he put his sword down.
"No fight? How will *this* look to the folks back in town?!
Mr. Dragon, I've promised a princess so fair
to come here and smite you, as brave princes dare."
"You know," said the dragon, "good Prince, you're all right,
and I'd like nothing better than to give you a fight.
For there's a *girl* dragon whom I, too, desire.
But for *her* to love *me*, I must once more breathe fire.
So, you see, Prince, I, too, feel the same way you feel.
We could both win our girls' hearts if we both make a deal."
So that night Prince Strongheart and the dragon, together,
gathered wood, twigs and sticks and some bits of old leather,
and made a large fire in the old dragon's hovel.
Then the dragon ate the fire with a pitchfork and shovel.

By morning the dragon was his old self again,

roaring fire and smoke with some help from a friend.

Then the two of them went outside into the light.

But both of them just stood there, not wanting to fight.

"I'm sorry, Dragon," said the Prince, "I can't fight you and such.

You're no longer just a beast, Sir, I like you too much."

"Thank you," said the dragon, "I feel the same way toward you.

But what of your princess? *Now* what will you do?

After all," said the dragon, "you told her you'd smite me.

Can you win her heart still, if you don't try to fight me?"

From behind the big tree came a voice shouting, "Yes!"

Then out walked the Princess in her long, flowing dress.

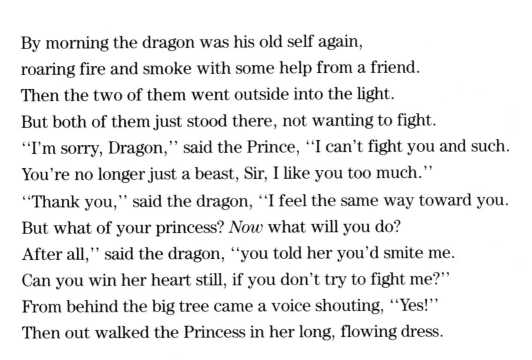

She had followed the Prince from her village below.
"Now, I know," said the Princess, "all I need to know.
You came here to fight, but the dragon was old.
And you could have slain him quite simply with his fire gone cold.
But you helped him instead, and for that I am sure
you're truly a hero with a heart strong and pure!"

So the Prince won the heart of the girl he desired.
The dragon got *his* wish, once more breathing fire.
And the dragon never did attack the village below,
never burned up the houses. No! Good heavens! No!
He could never do that to the Prince and his wife.
And the Prince and the dragon remained friends for life.

Now, I guess all fairy tales have a moral,
so this thought I leave with you:
The strongest heart and the bravest heart
is a heart that's caring, too.

I DON'T BELIEVE IN GOBLINS

I don't believe in goblins,
and I don't believe in gnomes.
I don't believe in ghosts and spooks
that come and haunt your homes.

I don't believe in monsters
or flying saucers from the skies.
I don't believe in anything
I haven't seen with my own eyes.

They're all BALONEY!
I *know* I'm right!
But, *just* in case . . . just, *but* . . .
Just in case I'm wrong,
I'm keeping both of my eyes SHUT!

A FAT MOUSE NAMED FRED

There once was a fat mouse named Fred,
whose tummy-ache kept him in bed.
Too much candy and jelly
and jam in his belly!
Fat Fred should have had cheese instead.

THE LUCKIEST MONKEY

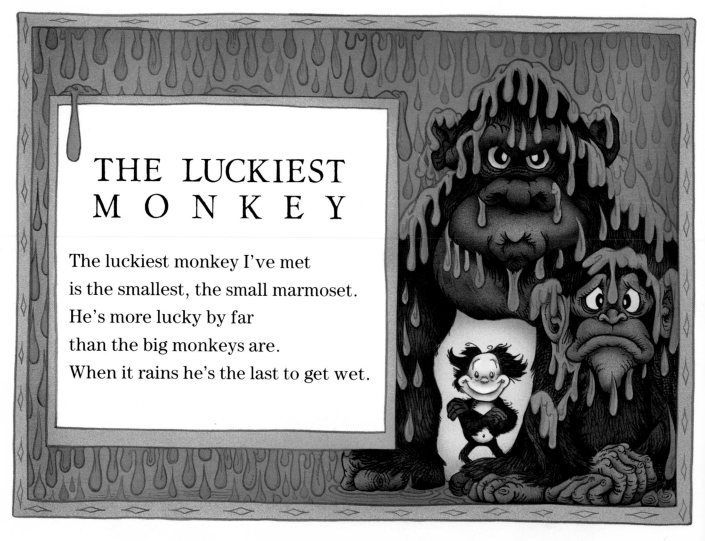

The luckiest monkey I've met
is the smallest, the small marmoset.
He's more lucky by far
than the big monkeys are.
When it rains he's the last to get wet.

THE · LATE · BIRD

The Early Bird always gets the worm,
it belongs to the Early Bird only.
But the Late Bird sleeps in his nest till noon
and gets the pepperoni.

WILLIAM THE RABBIT

William the Rabbit walks 'round on his ears.
Don't ask me why, but he's done it for years.

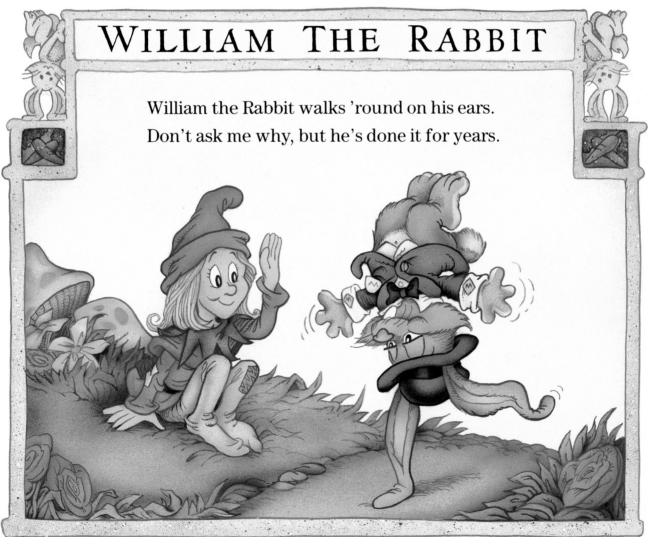

HAIL TO THE MOODLE

You've probably never heard of the thing called the Moodle,
which is kind of a cross 'tween a moose and a poodle.
It lives and it works on the top of Mount Hector
and its job is to be the Great Snowflake Inspector.
Yes, snowflake inspecting's the name of its game.
The Moodle makes sure that no two are the same.
From its perch on Mount Hector, the world's tallest peak,
the Moodle sees snow you won't see till next week.
It looks at them all as they fall from the skies,
checking each one for points and design, weight and size.
Then it opens its book and records with a doodle
every snowflake inspected by Inspector Moodle.
And, though it's rare, *if* two flakes *are* the same, then, you see,
it locks them away in a safe with a key.
It stops copycat snowflakes *before* they come down
and mess up our world and our country or town!
So, *hail to our hero!* Our *Inspector Moodle,*
who keeps all snowflakes different by using his noodle.

MY P^OG^O STICK

My pogo stick
goes hop, hop, hop,
hop, hop, hop,
hop, hop, hop!
Hop, hop, hop,
hop, hop, hop...

I don't know how
to stop, stop, stop.

MISS AMANDA'S ICE CREAM CONE

By far the tallest ice cream cone
in history was surely owned
by little Miss Amanda Hooper,
a super-duper *sixty* scooper.
She had: Vanilla Fudge, Pineapple Crush,
Mocha Swirl and Mango Mush,
Butter Almond, Chocolate Chip,
Tropical Fruit, Pistachio Flip,
Maple Walnut, Raisin Rum,
Tutti-frutti, Bubble Gum,
Orange sherbet, Lime and Lemon,
Raspberry Whip and Watermelon,
Crispy Chip and Chocolate Mint,
Cotton Candy, Peppermint,
Checkerboard and Fudge Supreme,
Peanut Butter, Butter Creme,
Amaretto Royal Fudge,
Pumpkin Seed and Slurpy Sludge,
Orange-Rhubarb, Heavenly Hash,
Strawberry Doughnut, Banana Bash,
Rocky Road and Marshmallow Mocha,
Pizza Mint and Tapioca,
Cantaloupe and Honeydew,
Maple Marble, Gummy-Goo,
Fudgy-Fudge and Rainbow Splotch,
Coffee-creme and Butterscotch,
Almond Raisin, Spicy Nuts,
Vanilla Pecan, Double-Dutch,
Candy Cane and Boysenberry,
Very Vanilla, Chocolate Cherry,
Guava Grape, Cranapple Chip,
Banana Twist and Licorice Whip,
Coconut Poundcake, Strawberry Slice,
Sugar Crunch and Lemon Ice.
But Amanda brought the whole thing back to the shop.
They forgot to put sprinkles on the top!

T A R   P I T   R O M A N C E

A LIMERICK OF MAMMOTH PROPORTION

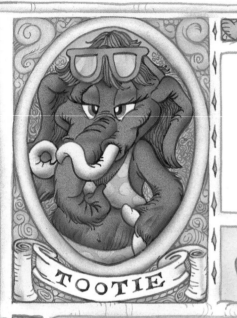

TOOTIE

There once was a mammoth named Tootie,
who they say was a real bathing beauty.
In the tar pit she plopped
with a big belly flop,
this cute bathing beauty named Tootie.

Then the tar started sticking to Tootie,
who was stuck from her trunk to her bootie.
And she couldn't get out
for no one heard her shout
'cause there was no lifeguard on duty.

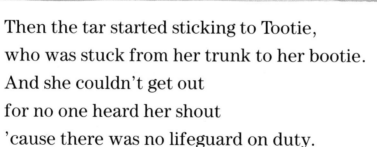

NO SWIMMING! LIFEGUARD ON PEANUT BREAK

Now, Tootie was stuckity-stuck,
all stuck in the muckity-muck.
Then the lifeguard came back
and he pulled her out, Jack!
Boy! You talk about luckity-luck!!!

Then Tootie and the lifeguard named Art,
were stuck trunk-to-trunk, heart-to-heart....
The tar hardened so soon
they got married in June,
since no one could pull them apart.

PRINCESS CLAIRE

Once upon a time in the Kingdom of Dare,

lived a king, and a queen, and a princess named Claire.

Princess Claire possessed a cuteness beyond compare,

except for one thing... she had *real* messy hair.

From the day she was born in her Dare royal home,

she would squeal, squirm and scream when approached by a comb.

Every time someone brushed it, Claire kicked them and cried!

Till their knees hurt so bad no one wanted to try.

Then the King called his own royal barber, McThrush,

to fix up Claire's hair with his gentlest brush.

So McThrush brushed her hair with his gentlest stroke,
but his brush hit a knot and his royal brush broke!
Then Claire screamed and the barber, McThrush, fled in dread!
And the broken brush stayed in the knot on Claire's head.
Princess Claire then descended the long palace stair
with McThrush's broken brush dangling still in her hair.
"Daddy, dear Daddy, kind Daddy," she said,
"please, tell all the barbers to *not* touch my head.
I do not like combs, even Barber McThrush's.
I do not like combs and I do not like brushes."

Then she cried till her eyes were all puffy and sore.
She cried till her father, the King, said "NO MORE!
From this day forward, not a person in Dare,
not a maid, nor a barber, nor a dresser of hair,
will *ever* touch your hair again!"
Then he called for his scroll and he called for his pen.
Then he sat down and wrote out a royal command
that was put on the scroll as the law of the land.
"Until I say otherwise, royal subjects of Dare,
no one is to go near my dear daughter's hair.
That is her wish, so then let it be done.
That is the law and, oh, *woe* to the one
who touches but one single hair on her head.
They'll be locked up for life in the Dungeon of Dread."

Then to make doubly sure that his daughter was safe,
he called for his soldiers and General Snafe.
He told General Snafe to go search all the homes
in the Kingdom of Dare and to seize all the combs!
And seize all the brushes! Each hairnet and spray!
Every shampoo and scissors and throw them away!
Then the army went out by command of the King
and searched out the brushes and seized everything.

Then they burned all these things in the Dare village square,
which shocked the whole village, but not Princess Claire.
For this whole thing was Claire's idea, right from the start.
"No brushing! No combing! Oh! Be still, my heart!"
Princess Claire said, "Now never again must I cry!"
Then days turned to weeks and a whole year went by.

Princess Claire's hair got longer and more and more mangled.

When she went for a walk, in her hair things got tangled:

first leaves, then twigs, then croquet sets...

then squirrels and birds and household pets!

Claire's hair now resembled a big tangled zoo.
And everyone else's looked just like that, too.
Since the soldiers had seized every brush, comb and scissors,
the whole Kingdom of Dare had a case of the frizzers!
All the dukes and their duchesses, every soldier and peasant,
had things stuck in their hair that looked very unpleasant.
And their tangles got tangled up with one another,
till you couldn't tell one from the next to the other.

The King himself called his new law a mistake,
when he found in his own beard a pig and a rake.
He cancelled the law and he called for McThrush
to climb into Claire's hair and go find his old brush,
the one left on Claire's head on that day long ago,
the only one left in the kingdom, and so...
McThrush jumped right in, much to Claire's great dismay,
and he didn't come out for a year and a day.

But finally he did! Good old Barber McThrush,
he came to the rescue with one single brush
to brush out the tangled-up Kingdom of Dare,
just one royal barber and miles of hair.
He brushed cows out of hair, he brushed birds out of ears.
And it sure wasn't easy; it took fifty years.
So the next time it hurts when your brush hits a knot,
be thankful you don't have the knots that Claire got.

MY M·A·G·I·C CARDBOARD BOX

I've got a magic cardboard box
that can be both a boat and a plane.
I drew the controls by myself with some crayons
on a day that I thought it might rain.
I keep it down in our garage,
right there next to my bike.
I can jump inside and float or fly
to anyplace I like.
I can set my crayon controls for "flight"
and rocket right up to the moon.
I can fly up even higher, still,
if I hold enough balloons.
If I want to sail the oceans,
then I set my controls for "float."
And I can be a pirate in
my magic cardboard boat.
Then I sail right back to my garage
after visiting strange, distant lands
in my super magic cardboard box
that I drew on with some crayons.

When the evening comes to the countryside,
on his swift, black horse, he makes his ride.
His dark outline is bathed in the light
of the ancient moon. He is The Knight.
He flashes his sword and he raises it high.
And his sword is so sharp it cuts stars in the sky.
And the stars light his way
as The Knight races by.
And The Knight never stops . . .
and nobody knows why.
It's a mystery to us and a secret he keeps:
why The Knight keeps on moving, why The Knight never sleeps.
But The Knight stops for nothing . . .
he stops for no one
as he races the moon
and is chased by the sun.
He is chased by the sun
as the hours rush by.
And the stars that his sword made
all fade from the sky.
And another day comes
with its light bright and clear.
And the day makes The Knight
and his horse disappear.
But, when once again
the Sun grows tired and dim . . .
if you watch the gray hills
once again you'll see him.
You'll see his black horse
that chases the light
when the ancient moon rises
again comes The Knight.

WHAT'S · IN · A · NAME?

Every little
breeze
seems to whisper
Louise.

But I don't
think a wind kin
whisper Rumplestiltskin.

K A N G A R O O S

Kangaroos never, ever should hop upside-down
when they do their hip-hopping about.
Because *if* kangaroos ever *did* hop that way,
then the one in their pouch might fall out.

NIGHT LIGHTS & PILLOW FIGHTS

Take a bath and get a hug,
toys and clothes left on the rug.
Fresh, clean sheets that smell so fine
from drying outside on the line.
Pajamas with feet with one toe showing,
pillow fights and night lights glowing.
A book to read, a rhyme or two.
A kiss good-night. An "I Love You."
Now get to sleep, you sleepy head,
and no more jumping on the bed!